MANNERS

ALIKI

GREENWILLOW BOOKS, NEW YORK

Library of Congress Cataloging-in-Publication Data
Aliki.   Manners / Aliki.   p.   cm.
Summary: Discusses manners and gives examples of good manners and bad manners.
ISBN 0-688-09198-9. ISBN 0-688-09199-7 (lib. bdg.)
1. Etiquette for children and teenagers.   [1. Etiquette.]   I. Title.
BJ1857.C5A39   1990   395'.122—dc20   89-34622   CIP   AC

For my mother,
Stella Lagakos Liacouras

MANNERS

WHAT ARE MANNERS?

Manners are the way people behave.

Manners are the way you treat others.

Thank you!

Good manners *GOOD MORNING!* make you nice.

They make others *Hi, Max!* want to be with you.

With good manners, you are polite. *Please have some.*

You are thoughtful and considerate. *I'll help!*

Manners are WORDS and ACTIONS that show others you CARE

WHAT BABIES DON'T KNOW

Babies are not born with manners.

They do not know how to say *Please!*

or *Thank you!* or *I'd like my Teddy!* or *I'm sleepy!*

Babies cry for things because they can't talk.

But babies grow into children, and learn.

They learn manners so others will want them around.

NOBODY LIKES TANTRUMS!

GREETINGS

How do you do?

Good Morning,
Mrs. Lambros.

Hello!

Please
come
in.

Please
have
a seat.

Would you
like a drink?

It was a
pleasure
to meet you.
Goodbye.

It was nice
to see you
again.
Goodbye.

Goodbye.
See you
tomorrow!

Have a
good
day!

ha
ha

WHAT ELENA KNOWS

Please
may I
lick the
bowl ?
I promise
to eat
all my
supper!

"Please"
goes a long
way.

For that,
Elena will
probably get
a cookie, too.

MANNERS LESSON #1

Aunt Bessie Doesn't Have to Know Everything

I'M SORRY

MANNERS LESSON #2

The Sand Castle

THE GRABBER

MANNERS LESSON #3

Too Loud Is Too Loud

LOOK AT DANIEL

DON'T YOU WISH YOU DIDN'T HAVE TO?

Here's a hanky, Daniel.

HOW ANTHONY ALMOST RUINED DIANA'S PARTY

Anthony never says hello.

He has no manners.

He embarrasses.

He makes fun.

He's a bad sport.

He cheats.

He bites.

He calls people names.

He grabs.

He tattles.

He throws food.

He's rude.

He didn't even say good-bye.

Nobody missed him.

He almost ruined my party.

But he didn't.

GOSSIP
and
WHISPERS

NOBODY'S PERFECT

OUCH

Here comes Alexa.
Let's ignore her.

Bad manners
and
bad feelings.

Is Alexa
going to go
home and cry?

MANNERS LESSON #4

At the Table

Seen but not heard.

MANNERS LESSON #5

Part One: Wrong Number

Part Two: Telephone Talk

MANNERS LESSON #6

Traveling

PLEASE, I CAN HELP

A lack of manners
in certain places
can bother others
and cause red faces.

GULP.

Don't
litter,
either.

PARDON AND EXCUSE ME

MANNERS LESSON #7

Sleep-over

Let's pretend.

About what?

You invited me to spend the night, and here I am.

Hi, Chris.

Do we get a snack?

That's not good manners.

I know. It's pretend. Do we?

I was just going to offer you one.

Here's a good game.

I want this one.

And then this one. At my house I always get my way.

I'm going to help with dinner.

I never help at my house.

At my house we always get soup, too.

You're not at your house.

Bedtime.

Already? I'm allowed to stay up all night.

I get the bed. You can have the floor.

Ha. I like the floor.

Ha Ha. Horrible, wasn't I?

You'd never get invited again.

Please can you come for a real sleepover? No more pretending!

Great. And we can both sleep on the floor!

EVERYBODY MISSES YOU

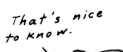

AND NOW FOR SOME ETIQUETTE

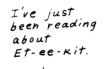

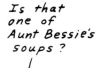

AFTER YOU

Wait for the hostess to begin before you do.

Offer others before you help yourself.

Wait for everyone to finish before you clear the table.

Let others enter before you.

Speak only after someone has finished.

Wait for your turn. It will come.

AFTER YOU means you think of others before you think of yourself.

THANK YOU AGAIN

A letter is like a book.
It can be read again and again and again....